CHAPTER 1

Ache in my heart

Lyrics from a song automatically evoking and making me sing, buzzing over and again to my hearing. They sing about an ache in the heart! An ache indeed, an ache with an injury and a trapped long overdue, deep breath, longing for fresh air and space. Open space is needed below the expanding sky and merely on the solid and stable line of longitude, to be able blow out in its full vast capacity. There is not much of a dream here in fact there is no dream of hope at all. They are singing about a dream. They mention a heap of a dream though here, for me, no hope for a split of next second. What is happening is unknown here and senseless, I am unaware of the direction to take the next step. Though, it seem as all clouded dreamy, dreadful sense of melancholic feelings crowded all around me, with thorny spikes, constantly distressing, irritating and aching me in and out. 'A heap of dream' is not a fore vision of wishful dream; it is as a mountain of lethal tussle and misery. Dreamy means the cloudy atmosphere of visibility, all around me. Where I am dragged forcefully, injured and pushed to the bottom of the hill of a mountain to climb up, while carrying responsibilities of delicate and innocents. The grieving sound of dee dee dee the very tone of sound that I keep singing is a self-criticism, to my failure of attempts and long endurance of suffering. Failure! Failure! Failure!

It is harder than it seems, deadly tough and irreversible. The fact is that it is far too harder than it seems. Where it sings with a hope to go to California, to me here, it is unknown, going where with an ache in my heart! A deep and long suffering ache in my heart! An ache in my heart poked in, with a deliberate planned deception, since a long ago, that I ignored and hundred per cent compromised with compassion. Then I was oppressed and deceived, I cried in grief and I was made vulnerable, still I tolerated and I continued with affection and compassion. Then I was made injured and that continued too, I voiced my grief. Despite I suffered and tolerated, I have been affectionate, compassionate, and encouraging to progress, while protecting innocents and vulnerable too, from harm, and there I had seek referral. I faced perpetuation of perpetration. I was more injured, vulnerable and I then and was served with more falsehood. Furthermore assaults to my heart! Here I am with an ache in the heart! The injury in my heart is unrecoverable. Surprise of my self-reflection I still remain compassionate! I do have sense of sensibility.

As they sing further along the lines, stating about hear and say, about a girl projecting love in her eyes and wearing a flower in her tresses. No in my case, no, no one told me that there is someone up there, with love in his eyes and flower in his hand or head. Too scary even to think of somewhere, to expect someone will be up there, somewhere who is honest and appreciative, with affection in his eyes! Let alone affection, honesty and fairness is expected does not exists. My sorrow of misfortune all I have met with misunderstanding, lies and deception. People all seem to know it all and right always. According to the proverb 'might is right. Might is always right! There I saw glimpse of compassion in eyes, that too momentary and unaccommodating.

The world seems at times is a trading market place of mutual gaining and giving, a negative way, where every issue seems to be a deal. Unjust and unfair dealing became a norm in world of business dealing and politics. It has been a custom of upper hand to be remaining upper level, by violating the human rights of fairness towards to lower hands. The acts of rights were introduced few centuries ago still seem to be played with. It seems like matter of knowing and understanding the game, even then might is required to play the game.

The acts of regulations here often violated and abused. Simultaneously, oppressed had been further oppressed under the mighty. Everyone here seems to play fair. They voice it louder than the action. It is not ignorable because in an aching situation even fair deal is unfair. Is it fair to give ache back in exchange of ache? Or is it to give Medicine in exchange of fair deal ache? Instead, should not it be to give medicine for the ache, not in exchange of ache? 'Dee dee dee', these very sound of saddened, that makes me think where is humane they call it? Here the suppressers treated with higher-level services and the oppressed are ignored or compelled to compromise.

We are proud of Britain's high quality services and appropriate system of rules and regulation. The service of Excellency is expected here and claimed are presented. It seems that the qualities seem to be open outwards with pride, to impress others rather than inwards. The same opened outwards door allowing devaluation to the system here. The services here made so authoritarian against vulnerability. Person employed abuses their even a little position against vulnerable and service users, although the position can be minor. They are Damaging, ignorant, and know it all! I failed again, against my conception of British high quality ethos of justice, humane and regard. Does that mean humanity and justice shall not be expect, if not regard and quality? Rules are been played with to misuse and abuse the systems. Individuals do wrong and deliberately play words to cover their backs instead of admitting, correcting and learning. Suppression and oppression is taking precedence due to lacking in adaptation of appropriate procedures.

Whereas in relation to the phrase 'with love in her eyes,' often people project like affectionate feeling through their eyes, they show their momentary desire through their eyes with fine talk, eagerly convey message of their inner passion and desperation through body language. They seek to meet their desire as they wish and the way they want it. They take control, begin to force in their way passionately screening with "affection". More often, these people are males than females. Among those few females fit in the above description, often do not succeed to screening well, though transparent, play continues. Where is love in it? And what is love? Is passion a wrong thing? Is affection a sign of weak heart? Affection does not desire control instead, it nurtures free, and according to Robindro Nath Tagore (Takur) 'Love does not claim possession, but gives freedom'. More he added 'love adorns itself; it seeks to prove inward joy by outward beauty. Love's gift cannot be given, it waits to be accepted'.

My profound perception proclaims; that the affection is strength in its-self, person nurtures it in him/her thrives. Simultaneously, affection is a weakness, it withers person's inner self and dysfunctions the heart under hurt feelings of self or the person of affection. It is a sign of weak heart because it compels person. Neither passion a bad thing, it enriches all desires, if that exercised with consideration and thoughtfully. Therefore, passion blends well into affection too.

Anyway, do eyes always portray affection, as it says 'with love in her eyes'? What is the communication rule here? Do we have codes of eye language or are we specific of signs? Obviously, eyes signal all emotions such as joy, sadness, compassion, desire and acceptance as well as affection. How do we differ? Tears of sadness are pretty obvious. Also tears of joy are distinguishable in relation to topic and moment. Can we take precise meaning out of eye language! Talking

CHAPTER 2

A moment of boost and gift of Compassion

A serendipitous wave, a calm invitation and sense of comfort in a pair of eyes, were filled with mixture of compassion and passion followed by questions, asking 'are you alright? How is he now'? The voice seemed to be it was creaking through a sheet of heart feeling of a little disappointment, with the feeling of warmth wrapped around it. Like when the plane cuts through the piece of cloud. I nodded, I could not talk. I was in a psychological and physical state of calamity like earthquake. Due to full of emotion, my eyes were filled with tears, that I was forcing to stuff them back in, simultaneously, my heart was screaming out, due to full of pain. Although, I did not expect to face these eyes of compassion and the voice of comfort, though, it seemed like a moment of still-spot during an earthquake.

A sense of comfort just for a split of moment seemed like soothing for me, though that was for a split of a second. It was like a break from tons of paining despair. May be like the state of drowning people. I heard the saying 'a drowning person seeks protection of even a minute debris of seaweed, with joy of relief.' I constantly had supply of strength, from my God (the sufficient)! Although there it felt like I was in a resentful mood, with some old sad feelings of disappointment and distrust. Again said 'sorry to hear that, please can I help with anything at all'? I replied blankly with 'thanks'! I was blank, apprehensive and self-restraining to prevent my emotional dispose. My emotion has become an accusation for me. Other than cause of concern, my emotional feeling has been unfairly judged and scrutinise for faulting.

The pair of eyes seemed to be if they were in desperate state, to express its inner sensation and to proclaim the state of its inner turmoil, while expressing its concern. Despite, I sensed its feeling and I was seeking to be soothing, I had to escape with discomfort because I was fearful of misplace words, wrong messages and out of place pushiness. Also I was fearful any likelihood of unpleasant demeaning assumptions, from other directions. Regretful feeling is not regarded with norm here. More and more people exercise, play with words, by twisting and tearing. And making assumption is at the top of the agenda for most people. Seeing feelings in eyes and body language has to be a game of assumption, with disgrace and scandal, rather than appraisal and to encourage. Instead of making assumption of someone's feeling, at least if they cannot leave it alone, to mind their own business, shouldn't they try to understanding that there is an innocent feeling of regret too, and shouldn't people treat such feeling with regard.

Prying attitude that was considered to be immoral seems to be replaced, modernised and updated with word 'analytical'. Far too many people became more and more so called "updated educated analysts". Quality cannot be taught! Mannerism cannot be injected into people! These qualities have to be saturated in and naturally produce from within.

Due to the Naivety of the ignorant' s ignorance and dismissiveness to sensitivity of my situation, I haven't been able to escape, the unpleasant demeaning and misreading of message, about the compassionate eyes, those were mixed with regret too. Any sorts of feelings that felt for others is very pleasant, whether its compassion, regret, disappointment or affection. Feelings are always felt. Like the old proverbial phrases of the Nature, the nature naturally sends the message of its acts, to the environment. The uprising sea wave roars and expresses its outburst. The essence of the flowers spread in the air to inform its blossom. In this human world although misreading and spreading of rumours takes grater part and causes upsetting and damages, contrary a word of or an act of compassion in an appropriate moment can be a gift of eternity and boost of spirit.

Where a word of compassion costs nothing, however, one of the laws of creation is, in a proverbial phrase it says, 'what goes up comes down' and literally does come back in many folds. A thoughtfully, planted seed germinates and grow in a crop, plant or a tree that produces goods.

Every deed germinates and produces in accordance to its nature. I just remembered the popular tale of Fleming family and Churchill family connection. Someone said that one day a poor farmer, somewhere in the north of England, while he was collecting woods for his earning and living. He heard a sick crying voice and noticed an ill child in a very bad sick condition, during the cold winter season, shivering in the cold outside. The farmer picked him up and took him under his shelter and nurtured him for the night. The next day, a cart pulled by his shelter, a well-dressed gentleman came out and entered into the shelter. Very thankfully, 'he addressed you have not only save my only son, you have saved my all entity. I am grateful to you so I want help you with a reward. Please take this money' forwarded some money. The poor farmer replied, 'I did not help him knowing that he is a rich man's son. I only did my duty of humanity therefore I cannot take this money'.

The rich man realised that the poor man is very dignifying character and he did not want to insult such person by offering little money anymore. The Richman noticed a boy over there, in the shelter and he asked, is this your son? The poor farmer replied 'yes'. Then the rich man said, 'not to repay you for taking care of my son, instead knowing your caring character, and because he is your blood, son of a noble father, he can do great services to others. Therefore, I want to take your son with me to allow him same education with my son, so he can do great service to others'. Many years later, by gaining education with the Richman's child, the poor man's child became Dr Fleming, who discovered penicillin and again the same rich man's child admirable, Sir Winston church Hill was cured by it. A good deed goes a very long way. What seed you saw that the crops you harvest. Also of course, there are contributions of other factors that too have an impact on it.

Going back to my emotion what had become an accusation for me during that period of time. There have been long on-going attacks from all direction against my thought process, with force and authority. I was pulled in different directions against my will despite I was refusing. A simple yes or no answer was not listened. A serendipitous entrant and an unexpected self-righteous manipulator became involved, in a family matter conference. Only one negative self-righteous character, within few minutes, demolished the entire contributory system, by creating a bizarre distressing atmosphere. My protector and the Serendipitous entrant was a witness to that. No wonder, how Asian countries are blindly muddled up with political exploitation and corruption. What is this, an era of political misguiding again? Instead of advancing and educating through globalisation, adapting to modern Western Conventionalism, and to promoting regards into integration, rather manipulation has been bought and allowed to be exercised here. Challenges of confrontation have been bought in to, to taste my strength. For what crime? For crime of being a victim under a circumstance, for endurance and for being considerate! People come back with a word 'sorry', after realising that further stress caused, due to falsifying and misleading the issue by ignoring and causing misunderstandings, because of not listening. My faith has been my strength, the greatest source of strength! I saw a glimpse of right from the wrong for a moment and felt hopeful with the complaining procedure that too was oppressed. However, a little deed of listening to crying voice is also a relief and hope that too can be comforting for a moment.

Advice and suggestions were forced onto me, without any validity. Lies and misleading seems to be taken the front seat here, and moreover, the truth falls not only far behind, actually drops down far below too. The manipulation became contagious, within the environment and among those involved, for months and years now. Simply this was one of the stages of reason for my emotional state. My emotion was further aroused later on by questioning of the serendipitous entrant, where I had matter of trust ability issue, while having to be cautious of not to allow any feeling of alienation. However, I failed maintaining the balance, as it says there is a limitation and I have hit my mark of limitation there. Still my faith is as strong as before because it confirms that I am a fallible ordinary human being, not a divine power of some sort. Word limitation reminds me that, the dishwasher repairer British Indian came to repair the dishwasher, he asked me 'what is wrong with it'. I replied 'I have no idea because I could not pull it out to have a look at it', he confirmed saying 'we all have our limits'.

After facing the bizarre atmosphere of manipulation and distress, I raised my voice of concern applying the appropriate regulatory procedures. Instantly, that was oppressed too with manipulation, falsifying and full force of power of controlling manners has been applied on with tactics. The power was played and continued, its impact continued too. At home, I met with further controlling dictation and abuses, despite being helplessly under controlled dictation of my protector, who is responsible to protect me and his duty is to nurture me with love and gentleness. Contrary all he served was anger, cheating and torture. Helplessly, I was seeking comforting shelter, for split of second and a moment of comfort and space. It seemed as if it was an imminent moment of stormy, thundery and windy weather approaching, from all direction and I was running around, from person to person, to alert their attention to the issue and the threat. I am telling people, all concerned what has happened. Am I heard? They want to know, asking questions saying tell me, tell us what happened. I retold, saying repeatedly, the same thing, over and again, feeling dreadfully exhausted, do they listen at all or just hear it? I was feeling giddy, weak and breathless as usual, with a half blurry vision, unaware of whom to trust, where and who is an ally. I was ill by exhaustion.

I was harassed by oppression of the manipulator, in front of my own protector (who is meant to be), then further the manipulator shocked me and lied, then covered up his ill, unprofessional and inappropriate manners, under a very polite and naïve comment of the serendipitous entrant. Later on, within few hours, with false implication he convinced my protector, that he is an ally. Ally for what, what is an ally needed for? I exclaimed, I am not on a battle or a war!

All seemed horribly scary, threatening and anti-integrate to me because I am here raising two kids, they are boys, here in Britain with Britain's ethical values and western cultures of to live and let live. Nurturing with teaching human Good Morals, respect of Britain's justice system, together with Teaching of Islam as well as although very little of Bengali Culture and heritage. I am encouraging understanding, tolerance, and indiscrimination of social inclusivity of all background. It is very much inappreciable suddenly to accept a comment from a stranger saying these people versus us. In his statement of us included the stranger him-self, who clearly demonstrates his low quality nature. Who are us? What is the relativity here? If something smells fishy then certainly there is something to do with fish.

Segregation has been evidently damaging. Some negative minded damaging characters' always have used the method of segregation in the mane of either culture of faith. I strongly proclaim that culture is in an individual. Each individual person holds a culture in its-self like nature. In regards to faith, worshiping God the creator does not require any authoritarian's permission neither restriction can deter the devotion.

These kinds of manipulators do not have a true devotion in them either. Culture what they call it, is their individual agenda, to fit their agenda in they play manipulation and create bizarre disruption. They learn words and policies to play with it. They read into feelings to use or to attack on it. Feelings have no regard to them other than for their self-centred motives. All they can do is abuse only. They cannot be comforting due to their self-righteousness ego.

Disturbances and chaos created in the atmosphere, simply to exercise authority and to dictate power of position, in a delicate, friendly family oriented environment, of one of the best and highly regarded ethical borough in West Midlands, not in a war zone of old fashioned rigid military combat zone. Despite suffering the feisty treatment, I called to alert all who were involved, against further potential damage by the manipulator. I was not concern only for myself though for the entire services. While I was leaving informing one person who is involved, the serendipitous entrant approached towards me and asked are you all right? Though very vague, it seemed to be caring, may be it was. Was it caring or curious? I only nodded to imply, yes. I had no guts due to embarrassment and lacking in energy to stop and talk. I was feeling very uneasy and I was unaware of its nature, also understanding was another issue that I hadn't with it, we vaguely knew each other.

I was very reluctant to talk to this person as well as it was ignorant in the past. For some reason, I was unable to voice out even little talk as greetings, due to my voice incapacity. No, don't get me wrong, it wasn't an unpleasant character at all, it seemed to have very good rapport with others and pretty focused towards to a certain crowd. Anyway, my voice triggered some kind of shrieking sound in certain environment, under stress. My decade long lost voice and talk ability was threatened at times, in fact most times. No, no, I do not have speech problems of any sort, except for triggered dry mouth issue. I talk like a radio people do say. Before I used to talk for hours with anybody or everybody whenever or whoever opened a conversation, or I used to initiate the conversation too, if the atmosphere seemed appropriate to me, without any sort of uneasiness. Going back to it, I heard the serendipitous talking many times, it speaks with a very casual and child friendly phrases. Oh yes, that suits well in his nature of profession. Suddenly it got involved in the above mentioned situation, at the same time as the manipulator. Due to a very unpleasant, unacceptable and inappropriate attitude, poor level of experience I had from the manipulator, I was not in a good frame of mind. I had nervous breakdown there with shock attack, due to his forceful dictating attitude. I was comforted with and care by two very caring women whom were involved too. May god blessed them both. When I saw the serendipitous entrant approaching, I had an uneasy feeling of awkwardness. However, I had to face this so I did. It made a comment with astounded expression at hearing my speech. Its comment made me to throw a blank silence glance at its direction (with warning of cautiousness for likelihood of threat of misuse of comments, though I was speechless). The comment was manipulated as I feared that would be. That was very a hurtful situation and distressing moment, not only disappointing and discomforting.

The entire issue and all comments of recording were manipulated, twisted and falsified. All attendees have noticed the misleading attitude and have commented on misleading recoding, inappropriate mannerism and poor dealing. Furthermore, the manipulator's incompetency acknowledged and addressed too, despite his faults pointed out, he continued with further misleading and falsifying the issue later on to a different crowd. Shame of such characters they cannot be corrected. They are very rigid and unwilling to approved methods of changes. This is where the word rebellious fit perfectly well. These types of individuals always seek power and abuse it. Power craver abusers have been granted with a position. Where does the manipulator fit in today's Bangladeshi politics? Bangladesh is running by women, dictating by women, in government the prime minister and the key ministers are women, and the opposition leader is a woman. He has disgraceful attitudes towards a woman! It makes me wonder sometimes, where to fit in! Here in Britain in this current diverse and century long integration society, people still here seems withdrawn from one and other. Some people playing word culture here, the culture in their terms does it link all personas from each category with similarity to one and other? No it does not. This is all about a push and pulls game. Culture does not link, it is the personality, interest and personal choices create the match.

And understanding creates comfort and both understanding and feelings encourages compassion.

Getting back to my grievances, personal and emotional injuries, I have been dragging along for a lengthy period of time, got heavier, has been hurting deeper at times, that I self soothe my condition through meditation of my inner compassion, mercy and for sake of innocent dependants.

I gain my strength to support, defend and to allow nurturing to prosper, to prevent from likely harm or potential threats. I ignored my emotional and general needs, all the way along, to be able to accommodate fully, the needs of dependants, others and the grievances giver too. God bless the caring human beings there were, who have spared comforting words. I was continued with facing similar hurtful incidents.

The giver of grievances always promised to be thoughtful and to change his attitude, as he knew it all though he could not deliver the promises. Instead, the giver of grievances, the protector played win, win, and game of talk smooth. Talking with confident and loud voice wins the entire battle. Once I saw in the professional counselling leaflet that 'abusers abuse, blame, tell lies, create criticisms and do press the faults on victim as well'. For a lengthy period of time, the faulting abusing method did not affect me as much, because then I was surrounded with non-political acquaintances there and this kind of attitude did not interest their personal motives, neither they were ignorant or manipulate able. My victimised status was admired silently by some fellow Asian and I saw sympathised smiles on faces with blessings, which always gave me strength and sense of normality.

I continued carried on with hope of next stage, next moments to be positive. Not for me at all for the sake of others. First and the foremost, for the sake of the grievances giver, to help him to come out of abusing acts and of his reasoning for angrily abuses, by soothing him with comfort, I have been encouraging and begging him to let his feeling out with his trusted friends, suggesting of available professional assistance. All three stages of methods, he dismissed his own ways. Soothing was appreciated with childish smooth words, sometimes with further anger, swearing words, oh, not towards me though on my face. Friends were his way of hiding his deeds and getting approval for his greatness of quality. And in regard to professional assistance, oh, dear me; greatest of all well-mannered understanding and time excuses due to work, very well allowed him to escape.

Talk smooth and crying for sympathy and understanding of his childhood issues. I compassionately gave in. Further aggravation and disturbances and someone has to be a target, even a baby, own beloved child, child that gives him moments full of pleasure with its blossoms. Hurt! More hurt returned with begging crying with sorry and promises of 'never next time'. Simultaneously, there was, the root and cause of abuses, the core and abuse encouragers, other extended abusers abusing too. Hope! Hope and mercy I nurtured. Mercy amazed I am tons and tons of mercy regenerated in me for outwards purposes only. I never had self-pity. Abused my inner strength! Overly exercise of tolerance, I have self-abused my-self too, I must admit. Feelings do hurt and too do soothe. My own compassionate feelings what generated within me for others, even that used to soothe me and boosts strengths in my-self.

I appreciate those acquaintances, local mothers of other children that came forward being friendly, with warmth and welcoming gesture. My uneasy feeling and unclear vision was difficult for me at times. Exhausted I was all the time. A toddler and an infant school aged child with demands of constant physical attention. Physical and psychological exhaustion I endured. Some caring natured persons (women) have engaged in and contributed a lot of warmth. One particular person cared and helped me, metaphorically to restructure my broken structure with a little communication and I became alive and norm. He who became my mentor and his eyes and voice had soothing inspiration for me. He spared time for me and he was responsive to me. I for good few years approached him and asked him for direction and assistance, and he at least spared few minutes of his time for me. Also I was very fortunate to have a great humane friend. The great friend of mine is still a dear friend who unfortunately is a very unfortunate person. Life hasn't treated her right, though she her-self treats everyone with care and regard. All these are my fellow Britain's co-inhabitants, not Muslims.

The current turmoil situation of mine emerged from the results of the misleading and oppression, and the manipulation of the issues by few people and their misuse of the position.

Distressing and exhausting it has been for a year, although no physical straining requiring, I am emotionally restrained at times, due to unnecessary pressures applied on me. The serendipitous entrant became controlling and pushy with its understanding and a lot of misunderstanding. Then it was apologetic later on. Then the wind changed its direction. It offered hand of friendship to shake hands with an offer displayed in its eyes.

I had to cautiously take back step to avoid a lots of unexplainable issues, to avoid misconception and misleading, I felt it would be best not to encourage towards its feeling, purely to avoid causing it any disappointments. It was persistent trying to impress me in different styles. Once it was disappointed when I did not compliment about its hairstyle. Well fashionable and trendy long my sons like style. I cut and style my sons hair, how they want it. Anyway, I remained consistent and avoided direct glance. Oh! NO! Suddenly the entire universe collapsed on me and pressed me down with multiple wounds. Entire life production of my effort and reason for my being has been crashed. I have to be strong to face, to deal, to endure and to help him to come out of all this with a right solution to get a hopeful result. My son ended in hospital with severe broken leg, he was in need of nurturing and support. I am selflessly running around like a headless chicken, with aching mind and body, giddy and stiff, all day and night between two children. There I met with more challenges.

The next day at school, it approached with compassionate feeling in eyes and comforting voice. It offered help though, likelihood of exclusion and harassment to minorities and individuals. Harassment could be unsettling and dangerous. On the other hand, to maintain a system to please all and to prove indiscrimination, to be, up to date with its European systems the government has to approve ways of lifestyles. Rightfully, a lot of criticism arises against these reformations of acts, from all direction and raising opinion against policy is rightfully democracy.

The current Middle East situation dragged on for a year now. Muslims practicing anti-Islamic actions, so called Muslims hypocrites they are, power cravers and abusers they all are. Do Arab nations' leaders and general people those are here in Britain, raise their voice of arrogance in speech reflect to them-selves in relation to this current situation! Teaching of Islam is not their teaching subject only, for them to just hold or claim teachers' role. All teaching is for learning and all learning is to put in practise. I wonder about these Arabs, are they all Muslims or just Arabs or Arabian? Shedding blood on the street of Arabian countries clearly reflect their level of Islamic learning and practises!

Muslim countries they want. In Pakistan, politics is a legitimate bribery and terrorism, democracy does not exist there at all. Pakistan is a field of terrorism, where harbouring, training and exercising terrorism within the country, bombing its cities and innocent public.

Anyway, Pakistan was created and named very thoughtlessly to fulfil the hunger of position cravers therefore consequently it is resulting to its mode. Muslim League was initiated procedural way, by Bangali Muslim for Muslims right during British rule, in 1830s by honourable Haji Shariatullah. The true history has been wiped off. Again some power craver abusers abused and changed its complete direction to satisfy their political greed. Oppressed their own people, deprived minorities tribes, decent public and fellow Good, moderate and genuine practising Muslims.

Ironically all these above indecent acts were carried out in the name of Islam. Islamic all inclusive legislative teaching, fair dealing, social justice, indiscrimination, rational, analytic, peaceful and tolerance has been ignored and abused by these so called Muslims.

Kaide Azam or Ali Jinnah, craved power and negotiated for Pakistan at any cost at the time of British departing India. He could not consider having a co-position with Nehru. He was adamant for his own power and position. To exercise authority and play power he needed fellow ordinary Muslims to protect him, praise his leadership, to be slaughtered and to slaughter others. Yes, Hindus also killed Muslims too. To me it does not justify killing by blaming Hindus killing Muslims. Namely Muslims began to indecent acts of all sorts. They wanted a Muslim country named Pakistan that is very 'Islamic or Muslim name'! Ali Jinnah himself did not have much of Islamic knowledge, neither was Practising much. Like some people, seems to act as they are great Muslim by hating or opposing non-Muslims other than by practising Islamic teaching. He could have consideration for sake of are up to something else. Later I discover most of them are liars and connected to cheating and immoral acts.

Some others had very certain understanding of my situation according to their judgemental attitude. A man had children from his late wife and remarried to a younger woman later on, they had an additional child from her. They were convinced that I was not a real mother to my first son and he was from his father's prior relation, because I seemed to have guarded my aging factor. Also he does not resemble me, he resembles to his father. To prove that they are right they are creating discomforting atmosphere to us. It is unbelievable that People waste lot of their energy on this kind unnecessary judgement. At l least white people ask or just try to find out and they go with the answer. These Asian, the minority of Pakistanis in this region of Britain are like Byzantine's army. Always as usual the negative minorities cause biggest impact.

Another factor here with majority groups of Asian Muslim people, a little basic Islamic essential learning that is instructed to be must, for their practises. They learning either they have neglected for too long and suddenly began to learn a little, or rigid with a little inexpensive understanding of a practise, and also influence of Bollywood movie scenarios gives them false sense of expertise of all topics.

With their little knowledge or understanding they begin to impose that on others, and here is a key contributory factor to their disregarding manner is assumption. According to an old proverb, 'a little learning is dangerous' that seems to apply in many cases here. People start to make assumption in all and every cases. Constantly make comparisons and assumptions, creating complication for straightforward people and they complicate topics. In this modern era people should be educated on all topics as much as possible, which is for every bodies benefit and to prevent people from causing disruption and harming each other.

Sharing knowledge is different to imposing because sharing knowledge confirms learning and is a positive thing for the society. Also raising conversation to be informative about topics and understanding is also a positive thing. Another issue here is mental condition of people, depression seems too common in people, more in Asian women due to unnecessary restriction verses ego conflict. Most people seem very hostile with ego and very pushy. Bias and judgemental damagers they are to them-selves and to others. Their comments are influential due to grouping support or their husbands, though negative. They are blinded with righteousness and are self-restricted with imposed pattern of manner on them though they are egoistic with these possessions. Once a Pakistani woman used to be a neighbour during our last residence said, 'trying to strike the balance'. I praised her with encouragement.

I had good sense of safe and caring environment; I felt I was belong too, once a decade and half ago. The environment was well diverse to me. I had good relationship and mutual understanding with all in the neighbourhood with regard. The others did not for some reason relate to each other. As

CHAPTER 4

Failure

Failure is a normal thing in life. We have to fail sometimes to understand the value of pass. Pass and fail are two factors seem to be present at every step of our life. We breathe easily without noticing, we take it for granted and it is an expected norm and one of our living right we believe. A right that we have come here with it, to live this life we are given. We breathe light every second. For any reason if we cannot breathe easily and it becomes heavy we divert our attention towards it and we draw attention of others too. This is not expected not be able to breathe easily, without any kind of even a minor pressure on it, therefore, it is unexpected. When an expectation meets with unexpected prevention which creates friction, the friction leads to a failure. Therefore, not being able to breathe due to complication means that there is a failure in the system.

Printed in the United States
By Bookmasters